SandCastle™

Baby
African Animals

It's a Baby

Meerkat!

Kelly Doudna

Consulting Editor, Diane Craig, M.A./Reading Specialist

ABDO
Publishing Company

Published by ABDO Publishing Company, 8000 West 78th Street, Edina, Minnesota 55439.

Copyright © 2009 by Abdo Consulting Group, Inc. International copyrights reserved in all countries.

No part of this book may be reproduced in any form without written permission from the publisher. SandCastle™ is a trademark and logo of ABDO Publishing Company.

Printed in the United States.

Editor: Liz Salzmann
Content Developer: Nancy Tuminelly
Cover and Interior Design and Production: Mighty Media
Photo Credits: iStockPhoto (Iwona Dost-Gorecka, Neal McClimon, Jean Paldan, Tina Rencelj, John Sigler, Nico Smit), Peter Arnold Inc. (J.L. Klein & M.L. Hubert, P. Wegner), ShutterStock

Library of Congress Cataloging-in-Publication Data

Doudna, Kelly, 1963-
  It's a baby meerkat! / Kelly Doudna.
     p. cm. -- (Baby African animals)
  ISBN 978-1-60453-157-2
1. Meerkat--Infancy--Juvenile literature. I. Title.

QL737.C235D68 2009
599.74'2--dc22

                    2008007016

SandCastle™ Level: Transitional

SandCastle™ books are created by a team of professional educators, reading specialists, and content developers around five essential components—phonemic awareness, phonics, vocabulary, text comprehension, and fluency—to assist young readers as they develop reading skills and strategies and increase their general knowledge. All books are written, reviewed, and leveled for guided reading, early reading intervention, and Accelerated Reader® programs for use in shared, guided, and independent reading and writing activities to support a balanced approach to literacy instruction. The SandCastle™ series has four levels that correspond to early literacy development. The levels are provided to help teachers and parents select appropriate books for young readers.

Emerging Readers
(no flags)

Beginning Readers
(1 flag)

Transitional Readers
(2 flags)

Fluent Readers
(3 flags)

SandCastle™ would like to hear from you. Please send us your comments and suggestions.
sandcastle@abdopublishing.com

Vital Statistics

for the Meerkat

BABY NAME
pup

NUMBER IN LITTER
1 to 6, average 3 to 4

WEIGHT AT BIRTH
1.2 ounces

AGE OF INDEPENDENCE
3 months

ADULT WEIGHT
2 pounds

LIFE EXPECTANCY
10 years

Meerkat pups are born underground. Pups nurse for up to two months.

Meerkats live in a network of burrows. Pups leave their burrows for the first time when they are three weeks old.

Meerkats eat mostly insects. They also eat scorpions.

Meerkats use their sense of smell to detect prey.

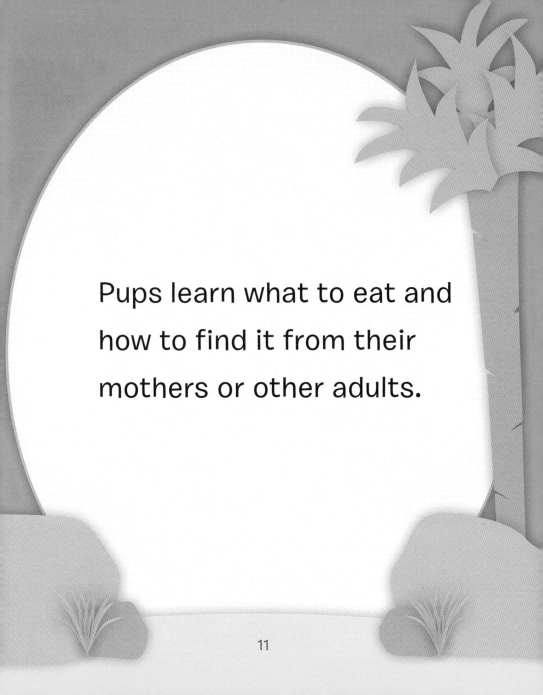

Pups learn what to eat and how to find it from their mothers or other adults.

Eagles and jackals are
the main predators of
meerkats.

Young meerkats are
even afraid of airplanes
flying in the sky!

One or two meerkats watch for predators while the other meerkats in the group look for food.

The look-out warns other meerkats of danger with a bark or a whistle.

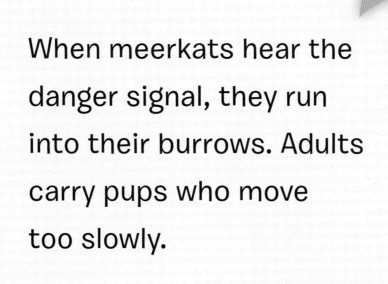

When meerkats hear the danger signal, they run into their burrows. Adults carry pups who move too slowly.

Most meerkats stay with their family group. They help raise their younger siblings.

If the group gets too big, some meerkats are forced to leave.

A meerkat uses its long, stiff tail to balance itself when it stands up. The tail acts like the kickstand on a bicycle.

Glossary

burrow – a hole or tunnel dug in the ground by a small animal for use as shelter.

detect – to sense, discover, or find out about.

expectancy – an expected or likely amount.

independence – no longer needing others to care for or support you.

network – something with parts that cross or connect, such as threads in a net, a series of tunnels, and computers joined by cables.

nurse – to feed a baby milk from the breast.

predator – an animal that hunts others.

prey – an animal that is hunted or caught for food.

scorpion – a creature with a long, bendable body and a poisonous stinger on its tail.

sibling – one's brother or sister.

signal – to send a message using a sound, sign, or device.

To see a complete list of SandCastle™ books and other nonfiction titles from ABDO Publishing Company, visit **www.abdopublishing.com**.

8000 West 78th Street, Edina, MN 55439

800-800-1312 • 952-831-1632 fax